SHAH JAHAN

& THE STORY OF
THE TAJ MAHAL

BY
Julia Marshall

ILLUSTRATED BY
Joan Ullathorne

HOOD HOOD BOOKS

Copyright © Hood Hood Books 1996

Hood Hood Books
29 Bolingbroke Grove
London SW11 6EJ

British Library Cataloguing-in-Publication Data
A catalogue record for this book is available from the British Library

ISBN 1 900251 08 6

Designed and Pageset by CW Typographics
Origination by Walden Litho
Printed and Bound in Italy

SHAH JAHAN

❧

& THE STORY OF

CONTENTS

SHAH JAHAN AND THE STORY OF THE TAJ MAHAL

THE OLD man got slowly to his feet and took a few steps across the room. He looked around him at the elegance and beauty of his marble surroundings. He had designed these very rooms, he had commissioned the best architects, craftsmen and artists so that his private quarters would be fit for the ruler of an empire. For that is what he had been just eight years before. He had commanded an army, governed the richest land in the world, he had been Shah Jahan, 'Sovereign of the World'.

Now, here he stood, a prisoner in his own palace, stripped of his precious jewels, dressed in plain cloth, an old man with a beard turned white. He had been in difficult situations before, he had spent half his life as a soldier fighting impossible battles against the most cunning enemies, but now he was powerless. He was too old and disheartened to face his current enemy who was none other than his very own son, Aurangzeb.

The old man, Shah Jahan, shook his head, fingered his white beard and held out the letter he carried so that he could read it once again. His hand trembled as he read the words. It was not the first painful letter he had received from his traitorous son, Aurangzeb. He could hardly bear to think of the previous letters that had announced the deaths, one by one, of so many of his beloved family – even his favourite son Dara. The old man could still remember the sorrow and anger that had flowed like fire through his body when he had heard how Aurangzeb had ordered his own brother, Dara, to be put to death by having his head brutally hacked from his body. That had been several years ago, but the old man's sadness was still as great.

Shah Jahan, felt his body grow weak. He was tired, he no longer had the strength to struggle in this life. He seated himself and once again read the letter. The words were like needles sinking into his flesh, rousing it once more to life. This was too much, he would not accept it. This wretched son of his, this Aurangzeb was going too far. Not content to slaughter his own family, imprison his father and strip him of all he held precious, he was now demanding the pearl prayer beads with which Shah Jahan said his prayers. If it was the last battle he fought, Shah Jahan would not hand over that rosary. His prayers were too precious to him now that he had lost everything and the beads, made of pearls so perfect, reminded him of how important beauty had been in his life, even amongst all the fighting and bloodshed. No, Aurangzeb would never touch these pearls. Shah Jahan would rather grind them to dust than allow Aurangzeb's fingers to soil them. He would write his son a letter and tell him just that. He would let him know that he would not be allowed to treat his father so cruelly. He would show him that Shah

Jahan was not afraid of his own son.

Getting to his feet, Shah Jahan searched the room for writing materials, muttering to himself as he opened drawers and chests in his search. No, there was nothing there that he could use. Summoning a slave standing on guard outside his room, Shah Jahan ordered him to call his daughter, Jahanara, to come to him. Within a few minutes she arrived, wearing a sari of blue silk woven with gold thread which rustled and gave off a rich perfume as she walked. She carried a silver dish of ripe grapes and scarlet pomegranates which she placed before her father.

"How are you Father?" she said with a smile, her voice calm and soothing.

"I am a sick old man," he replied, impatiently, "but I will not be treated as if I am worthless and insignificant. I need to reply to this letter from your brother, Aurangzeb, and yet I can find no paper and no pen."

The smile faded from Jahanara's face.

"I'm sorry Father, but Aurangzeb has forbidden you to have any writing materials."

"How can he, what right has he…" the old man stormed, but his voice faded away as he met his daughter's eyes. They had no need to speak the words, they knew that he was now a powerless prisoner. Tenderly, Jahanara put her arms around her father and stroked his white hair, trying to comfort him.

"Why don't you eat some of this fruit, Father. Look, have you ever seen such beautiful pomegranates? They are just like jewels."

But Shah Jahan shook his head.

"I have no appetite, daughter. I think I would like to be left alone now."

Jahanara bent her head and kissed her father before leaving the room, her silks rustling. Watching the movement of her body and the shine of her dark, smooth hair, Shah Jahan thought how much she reminded him of his beloved wife, Arjumund Banu, whom he had called Mumtaz Mahal, the Chosen one of the Palace. She had died when she was only thirty-nine giving birth to their fourteenth child. For Shah Jahan her death had turned the whole world into a house of mourning and his shiny black beard had become one third white in just a few days. In the thirty-four years he had lived since her death, he had often longed for his Mumtaz Mahal. He had always imagined that they would grow old together, ruling their kingdom and living in peace with their children. Now, more than ever, he wished that she were alive to comfort him in his sorrow. She may have been able to prevent his imprisonment. She would have spoken to Aurangzeb, pleaded with him for the lives of his brothers and nephews. Shah Jahan could not believe that Aurangzeb could ever have disobeyed his mother with her fine, strong looks and her gentle ways.

Shah Jahan now raised his head and looked from the window of his beautiful marble prison. There, across the bend in the river Jumna, he could see the Taj Mahal, the memorial to his wife which had taken twenty-two years and twenty thousand workers to build. In the soft evening light, the marble of the Taj Mahal's perfect proportions gave off a hazy radiance that made it look almost transparent, as if it might at any moment dissolve like a ghost and vanish. Shah Jahan kept his eyes fixed on its beauty, reminding himself that it symbolised the immortality of his wife and the life that awaited all people once their struggles on earth were over. But he could not contain his sorrow. He was still here, trapped in this room, held prisoner by his son. His pain broke from him in a great roar which echoed throughout his marble quarters, sounding like the cry of a wounded animal.

As his voice faded and silence filled the room once more, Shah Jahan heard a scuffling noise coming from the corner of the room, the sound of small feet running across the bright woven rugs. "A mouse!" Shah Jahan exclaimed indignantly, "a verminous rodent in my presence." Forgetting his age, he rose quickly to his feet and tipping the fruit from the heavy silver bowl, he raised it above his head, intending to crush the mouse. But all of a sudden his anger seemed to leave him and his arm dropped harmlessly to his side. The mouse had not moved. It raised its small pointed face to him, its round eyes seeming to look directly and fearlessly up at Shah Jahan.

"Well, you're a brave creature," Shah Jahan said out loud, laughing to himself and feeling only a little foolish to be addressing a mouse. "A real little soldier to be so fearless in the face of death." He placed the silver bowl back on the table and seated himself. Still the mouse did not move, but remained crouching among the grapes and pomegranates scattered over the rich colours of the rug, watching the old man with a serious expression.

"Well, you were taking a risk," Shah Jahan told the mouse, "gambling with your life. For you know, I fully intended to kill

you. It would have meant nothing to me. I have sentenced many men to be trampled to death by elephants. I have watched from the balcony of this very room as elephants fought each other. So what should the life of a mere mouse mean to me, Shah Jahan, Sovereign of the World?"

The mouse sat and looked and twitched its whiskers. Shah Jahan nodded his head gravely and spoke.

"Well, you might say, that I am no longer the Sovereign of the World, for what would the Sovereign of the World be doing talking to a mouse? But you see, mouse, although I shudder to hear myself say it, I who have been so powerful and have held the lives of whole armies in my hands, I find that you and I have things in common. We are both at the complete mercy of those more powerful than ourselves. I am now subject to my son, and you are subject to me. I can sympathize with you, mouse. I know what it is to suffer the reversal of fortune, to feel my very existence hanging in the balance. And I am not the first of my family to be in such a situation. Of those who have gone before me, many have felt fate pricking at their heels. So, I have decided not to kill you, but instead I'm going to tell you something about my life."

SHAH JAHAN TELLS THE STORY OF HIS ANCESTORS

So Shah Jahan sat, his hands moving every now and then over his white beard, his eyes gazing into the distance, out through the window of his marble prison, focusing on the majestic beauty of the Taj Mahal. His mind was free to wander over years and centuries gone by and while he spoke, he forgot for a moment that he was a powerless old man speaking to a small brown mouse. He remembered instead the glorious history to which he had greatly contributed as the fifth Mughal emperor of the mighty kingdom of India.

"I am the descendent of the Great Timur who the Persians called Timur-i-Leng, Timur the Lame because of his limp. But this did not prevent him from becoming mighty and feared, the 'Shadow of God on Earth'. It was he who first conquered India, although he did not stay there to make it his kingdom. When I was born in 1592, the planets were arranged in exactly the same order as at the time of Timur's birth and the court astrologers predicted that I would be a child who would outshine the sun. I was born in the same month as the prophet Muhammad and from the beginning great things were expected of me. It seemed that I was a chosen one and I wore my destiny like a rich cloak wrapped around my body.

"I was my grandfather Akbar's favourite and as a boy, he called me Shah Baba although my given name is Khurram. Shah is the name given to a ruler and Baba means father, so the name showed both his esteem and affection for me. My grandfather Akbar was more a father to me than my own father, Salim or Jahangir as he was later known when he became emperor. It was Akbar who decided that I should be taken from my mother, who was an Indian princess from the court of Rajasthan, and given to one of his own wives, Rugayyah Sultan Begum. She was childless and she loved me more than it was possible for any natural mother to love her son. And I returned her love. My own mother was consoled for my loss with a magnificent necklace of pearls and rubies.

"As a boy I was well instructed in the Muslim faith. From the age of four I studied languages and the art of writing. But I always preferred shooting, riding and fencing. With my grandfather, I spent hours discussing guns, horses and elephants and he filled me with stories of the triumphs and downfalls of my ancestors.

"Babur, who was my great-great-grandfather and the first of our family to rule India, knew what it was to suffer. He lost his beloved kingdom of Samarkand and was driven into the desert. There he and his men were forced to eat the flesh of dogs and donkeys while his horses ate nothing but wood pulp. But his fortune changed and he conquered India and carved out for himself a far greater kingdom than the one he had lost.

The map shows labels: Bukhara, Tashkent, Samarqand, Kashi, AFGHANISTAN, TIBET, Delhi, Agra, INDIA, BAY OF BENGAL

"Babur's son, my great grandfather, Humayun also knew what it was to lose a kingdom he had inherited. He was unable to control the greed and ambitions of his brothers and the kingdom that Babur had so fearlessly conquered began to fall apart. Humayun was driven from the land that was rightfully his. With his new wife, Hamida, who was only fourteen at the time, he spent two years being chased across the hot, bleak desert of Rajasthan. At one point they were forced to retrace their steps across two hundred miles of desert at the hottest season with their enemy, the son of the Raja of Jaisalmer, moving ahead of them, filling in the wells with sand. Humayun and Hamida with their followers had to live on wild berries and the flesh of asses. They had no pots and had to cook their meat in their helmets. Hamida was now expecting a child and suffered from this harsh way of life. She longed for the cooling, scarlet fruit of the pomegranate. Of course no such thing could be found in the heat of the desert. But just at this moment, they happened to cross paths with a merchant who drew from the bottom of his saddle bag one large, juicy pomegranate!"

Shah Jahan laughed to himself at the memory of this tale, and the mouse moved so that it sat upright on its haunches just in front of one of the pomegranates that had fallen to the floor when the old man had grabbed the silver bowl. The movement caught Shah Jahan's attention. He withdrew his gaze from the distant Taj Mahal and focused on the little brown mouse. He reached out his hand and picked up the red fruit. His fingers brushed the whiskers of the mouse as he did this, but still the mouse did not run away and instead sat watching Shah Jahan intently. The old man broke the fruit in two, releasing the succulent little seeds, red as rubies. Placing a few of these in the palm of one hand, he held them out to the little mouse who took one of the seeds and, holding it firmly in its pink paws, began to nibble at the red flesh.

"So you see, little mouse," said Shah Jahan, "how fortunes can change. You can never predict God's will. My great-grandmother found fruit in the desert and gave birth to my grandfather Akbar who in his turn ruled this great land. And you, little mouse, who sit so fearlessly in my presence, enjoying this fruit, it could have been your fate, just moments ago, to end up crushed beneath a silver bowl. As for me, I should not forget this lesson either. I have studied the lives of my ancestors. Babur's memoirs lay bound and treasured in the royal library throughout my reign. I no longer have access to them, but I have read them so often that I remember almost every word. My father also recorded his life and presented me with his writings. I should know only too well that life does not move in one unbending straight line, but bends and dips and curves like a great river, like the Jumna I can see from my window.

"My family have lost and conquered land, known triumph and defeat. They have known how to suffer and have also experienced great riches. Oh, my little mouse, if you could have seen what jewels came into my possession – the great diamond that Babur was presented with by the family of the Raja of Gwalior when first he entered this city of Agra. A diamond so large it was like a mountain of light and Babur himself said that its value would provide two and a half days food for the whole world!

Now all my jewels are gone from me, taken by my son, and I have only these prayer beads left.

"We have also been known for our cruelty, we rulers of India. We have killed many men in our battles for land and have built towers with the decapitated heads of our enemies. Things have gone badly for those who disobeyed or sought to betray us. Many have been sentenced to be crushed beneath the feet of elephants. Akbar, who was a great hunter and liked his sport to be as dangerous as war, roped wild elephants, faced tigers on foot and hunted with cheetahs whose coats were studded with jewels. He could be as swift and cruel in dealing out justice as he was when pursuing the enemy or his prey. He once cut off the feet of a man who had stolen some shoes. My own father, Jahangir, when faced with the rebellion of my elder brother Khusrau along with two of his friends, had these two friends sewn into the wet skins of a freshly slaughtered ox and an ass, head and ears included. Dressed in these skins, they were seated on donkeys and made to ride around the city all day. The hot sun dried the skins so that they shrank and one of the men suffocated and died.

"Yes, my family have been capable of cruelty and destruction, and yet we have also been generous with gifts and forgiveness. The wives and children of our enemies have, in most cases, been treated with kindness and escorted to safety unharmed. And you yourself, little brown mouse are witness to my generous behaviour. But more than mere pardons and generosity, we have filled our kingdom with beautiful creations. Under the reign of my family, India has nourished art and music and literature. My greatest

love apart from that which I held for my family – my beloved Mumtaz Mahal, my favourite son Dara and my beautiful Jahanara, has been for architecture. And now as I gaze from this prison towards the Taj Mahal, I find a promise of freedom from all my sorrows in the beauty of its marble dome."

Again Shah Jahan bent down and loosened some plump seeds from the broken pomegranate, offering them to the mouse. Smiling, he said, "so, my little brown creature, I am offering you these as a gift and in return you will listen to my story and how I came to build that most perfect of buildings."

SHAH JAHAN'S SUCCESS AS A SOLDIER

"AS I have told you, I was born with a great sense of destiny. Even though I was the third son of my father, I believed that I would one day sit on the throne and be ruler of all India. This belief was made even stronger when, at the age of thirteen, I sat with my grandfather Akbar watching an elephant fight which had been arranged between an elephant belonging to my father, Salim, and an elephant of my eldest brother Khusrau. Young as I was, I was still very aware of the rivalry that existed between these two. The struggle for the throne could never be absent from the minds of any of our family. My father's elephant, which was his favourite and his strongest, won the fight, but a battle broke out between his supporters and my brother's. I was sent by Akbar to put a stop to such undignified behaviour and from that moment I was aware of a certain power I held over both my father and my brother – even though I was still a mere boy.

"The death of my grandfather, Akbar, when I was thirteen, filled me with deep sorrow. I thought even then that should I become

ruler of this vast kingdom, I would try and follow his example. He had done so much that was good such as building roads and his great fort at Agra. He also strove to bring all the various people of India under one law so that they might all feel an allegiance to his rule, whatever their religion. When he died it left a great gap in my life.

"When my father, Salim, came to power, he changed his name to Jahangir, 'Seizer of the World'. I watched his struggles against my elder brother Khusrau who he finally had blinded so that he would no longer be a threat. The blinding was carefully done and my brother recovered half of his sight, but he was a subdued and broken man. I became my father's favourite and, when I was sixteen, he gave me the territory of Hissar Firoz and the right to pitch a red tent. Both of these privileges belonged to the heir to the throne.

"It was soon after this that a Persian widow came to court as lady-in-waiting to Salima, one of my grandfather's widows. She was a great beauty and very talented as a poet and designer of dresses. She set the fashion among the harem ladies who tried to copy her style. She was also a great huntress and shot tigers from a closed *howdah*, like a small tent, on top of an elephant. One time it was said that she used only six bullets to kill four tigers. My father could not resist her charms and fell deeply in love with her. After four years she agreed to marry him and became his Queen, his Nur Jahan, the light of the World. Her father, Ghiyas Beg was my father's chief minister and her brother, Asaf Khan was second only to his father. So this Persian family became very powerful at

court. Fortunately for me, Nur Jahan seemed to hold me in great favour and treated me with kindness.

"When I was fifteen, I met the daughter of Asaf Khan, Nur Jahan's own niece. Her name was Arjumand Banu and I was captured by her beauty and gentleness. She was destined to become my Mumtaz Mahal, the Chosen one of the Palace, but I had to wait five years before I married her. From the beginning of our marriage we were devoted to each other and were seldom separated. She followed me when my father sent me on dangerous campaigns to subdue uprisings in the kingdom and always she advised and comforted me.

"I was able to conquer the territory of Mewar which even my grandfather, Akbar had been unable to do. To succeed, I had to destroy much of the surrounding countryside so that my enemies would be forced to surrender through lack of supplies. My own troops suffered hunger along with the enemy, but we defeated them at last and I brought the royal prince from the senior house of Rajasthan back with me to profess loyalty to my father, Jahangir. Just two years later I was sent to the Deccan in the south of India where I subdued several rulers and brought back large sums of money and chests of jewels to my father. When I presented him with this treasure, he came down from his *jharoka* – the palace balcony from which he greeted his people, and poured a tray of jewels and another of gold over my head. It was a moment of great triumph for me when my father announced that I would now be known as Shah Jahan, Sovereign of the World. He ordered a chair to be placed near the throne so that I might sit in his pres-

SHAH JAHAN: THE STORY OF THE TAJ MAHAL   21

ence which was indeed a great honour. Nur Jahan herself gave a victory party for me and all my harem. It was magnificent and lavish, costing more than a thousand rupees and she presented me with a jewelled saddle and a turban decorated with rare gems."

Shah Jahan's voice had grown light and young as he told of his victories and the wealth they had earned him. It was no longer the voice of a tired old man, but one of a young warrior and the mouse stopped nibbling on the pomegranate seeds and seemed to prick up its ears to listen. But, as his words faded, Shah Jahan gave a deep sigh filled with regret. "Oh," he said, "even though I know that things must change and that it is God's will that they do so, I cannot help but feel great sadness over the turmoil that my life was thrown into in the years that followed. From being a young man, the favourite of my father and his Queen, blessed with wealth and success, I steadily lost favour until I was at war with my own father. He no longer honoured me with the title Shah Jahan, but called me *Bi–daulat*, the Wretch." Shah Jahan's voice was once again that of an old man, made heavy with the cares of the world. Slowly he stretched out his hand and with one trembling finger, he touched the head of the little mouse as if blessing him. Again he sighed deeply.

"I have been over it so many times," he said, "locked away in my prison, betrayed by my own son. I have thought back over the years and wondered how it was that I too, rebelled against my father. Jahangir, the Seizer of the World, was growing old, made weak by too much alcohol. He had been a good emperor, but was now so much under the influence of his Queen, Nur Jahan, that it could be said that she was in fact the real ruler. At this point she seemed to change before me. Perhaps she sensed my ambition and strength and feared that if I became emperor, there would be no place for her. I can only guess at her thoughts, but I could see that she no longer favoured me. Instead, she took my younger brother, Shahriyar, under her protection, marrying her daughter to him in a lavish ceremony. When I was ordered, once again, to go south to the Deccan to put a stop to further uprisings, I was reluctant to go. I no longer trusted Nur Jahan and with my father's health failing I feared what might happen while I was so far away from court. Full of misgivings I left, taking my half-blind elder brother, Khusrau with me. I was never to see my father again."

SHAH JAHAN'S STRUGGLE FOR THE THRONE

"I SPENT more than a year fighting and suppressing my enemies in the south and I built for myself a seat of power with strong troops. It was then that I was sent news that my father was again seriously ill. Being so far away from him, I am ashamed to say that I panicked, fearing that I may lose my claim to the throne. I acted in a way that I fear may have been the start of all my present misfortunes. I had my elder brother, Khusrau, killed."

It seemed to Shah Jahan in his guilt that the mouse was staring accusingly at him with its shiny round eyes. "You must try to understand," he said quickly. "It may seem that a half–blind brother could be no threat to the throne, but there were those at court who pitied him, and he was not without intelligence and charm. There were certainly some nobles who supported him. I could not take the risk. My whole life, I had been moving towards the one goal of the throne of India, and I would not allow anyone, not even a brother, to stand in my way. But I see now, that with that one ruthless act, I set in motion a chain of events that eventually resulted in my imprisonment here in Agra, and the loss of so many of my family.

"The killing of my brother was in vain. It brought me no closer to the throne. My father's health recovered in time for him to face the threat of the Persian, Shah Abbas, who was threatening Kanahar, one of our richest trading posts. Jahangir ordered me to join him in this common struggle with all my troops; but I refused, not wanting to leave the powerful base I had made for myself in the South. My father and his Queen called this a rebellion and troops were sent south to pursue me. I, who had been my father's favourite, had become his undutiful son, labelled as a wretch.

"For three years, I was pursued by troops led by my younger brother, Parwiz and a general called Mahabut Khan whom I knew to be a very talented soldier. For all these years, I was accompanied by my loyal Mumtaz Mahal, who bore all the suffering and discomfort without complaint. I grew to love her during that time even more than I thought possible. At last, tired out by this life of constantly running from an army, I established some sort of agreement with my father. I surrendered to him two fortresses that I had captured and sent him my two sons, Dara – who was then ten years old – and Aurangzeb who was only eight.

"My father, believing that now, in his old age and with his health failing, he deserved some peace, moved to Kashmir. This had always been a favourite place of his because of its beautiful gardens. Here, away from the scorching heat, there were fountains and pools that made their own peaceful music. It was here that my father chose to await his death.

Mumtaz Muhal

"At this stage I was joined by the General Mahabut Khan. He had spent three years trying to capture me, but now he became my ally as he too did not trust my father's Queen, Nur Jahan. As soon as Asaf Khan sent us news that my father had died, we moved with our troops towards Agra. I was in a strong position, but still I wanted to take no risks and now I must confess that I ordered Asaf Khan to arrange the death of my younger brother, Shahriyar who had been favoured by Nur Jahan. I also had two of my nephews and two cousins put to death so that they could not threaten me. Once again, I had set a pattern marked out in blood that my own son, Aurangzeb has now followed.

"At last, in 1628, when I was thirty six years old, I entered Agra riding on my favourite elephant and mounted the throne. I never doubted that this was my right and that God had willed that I should be ruler of India. I did not allow the deaths of my brothers and relatives to bother me. I forgot all about them in the happiness I felt at achieving my goal. At last I was able to make my Mumtaz Mahal a queen. I was generous with my father's Queen, Nur Jahan, giving her money and allowing her to retire to build the tomb of my father at Lahore."

THE DEATH OF MUMTAZ MAHAL & THE BIRTH OF THE TAJ MAHAL

"For almost two years my family knew a peace which they had not known for more than six years. My Queen and I lived in lavish style here in Agra. But all too soon, that peace ended and once more I had to travel south to the Deccan to subdue the uprisings. As always, my Mumtaz Mahal came with me, but to my great sorrow, she died on our journey while giving birth to our fourteenth child. Before she died, I promised her that I would never have children with another woman and that I would build the world's most beautiful memorial over her grave. Both of these promises I kept.

"For two years I lived in mourning, wearing plain clothes, without rich food, without music. I had been a soldier all my life, but now I turned away from battle and left all the campaigns to my four sons. My Mumtaz Mahal was dead and so I concentrated on another love, my love of architecture.

"My first interest was to fulfil the promise I had made to my wife and I began work on the Taj Mahal. I was determined that this building would be so magnificent, so beautiful, that anyone looking at it would not be reminded of the death of my Mumtaz Mahal, but of the eternal life into which she had passed. The tomb of my beloved wife would be an earthly paradise, a symbol of that which awaits all those faithful to God.

"I did not believe that any one architect would be good enough for such a creation, so I hired many to submit their various designs to me. I had many wooden models made before I at last decided on the perfect plan. No expense was spared, five million rupees were spent on the building alone. This did not include the cost of materials, the tons of marble and the cases of gemstones.

Around the tomb of my Mumtaz Mahal are forty-two acres of gardens planted with flowers and trees of all varieties. There are fountains and canals that fill the air with their own music. The garden is surrounded by a red sandstone wall full of galleries, pavilions and towers. The main entrance to this paradise – I can find no other word to describe its beauty and peace – is through a huge gateway, thirty metres high. This gateway is also made of red sandstone, but it is richly decorated with patterns of flowers made from gemstones inlaid in white marble and inscriptions from the Qur'an inlaid in black marble.

"The memorial to my beloved wife is cased inside and out in white marble. It surprises the eye of anyone who looks at it, seeming at first to be made of moonshine, light and airy; and yet its tremendous size gives it weight and grandeur. It is a building that puzzles people, always holding back its secret as God hides from

us the mysteries of life until He chooses to reveal them.

"The huge dome, forty four metres high, stretches over the body of my Mumtaz Mahal as heaven stretches above the earth and four tall minarets rise from the surrounding white marble like a magnificent frame. The outside is ornamented with colourful inlays of sculpted flowers and inscriptions from the Qur'an, but all this richness is not allowed to lessen the purity of the white marble itself. I went often, at many times of the day, from this fort to the tomb, travelling by boat down the Jumna to gaze upon the marble and see how the colours of the decoration enhanced its beauty as the light played on its surface. At these moments I was reminded of the beauty of my Mumtaz Mahal whose deep coloured lips and cheeks and dark shining eyes were mere reflections of the purity of her soul.

"I will never again see the inside of this tomb, but I planned it so carefully and I have spent so many hours in it, that I will always carry the picture clearly in my mind. I hope that when my life comes to an end, it will be my resting place just as it has been the resting place of my Mumtaz for all these years. I had this tomb built, like earlier tombs at the time of my ancestor Timur himself, in the form of what is known as the 'eight paradises'. Eight chambers surround a larger one. This larger chamber is eight-sided with two stories. In the lower one, the eight sides are outlined with bands of inlaid calligraphy and magnificent sculpted flowers. These flowers are symbols of the beauty offered to the faithful in paradise. Right in the middle of this main chamber is a marble screen, also eight-sided and two metres high. It is behind this screen that my Mumtaz lies."

Shah Jahan was now silent for a while as he gazed out of his window at the dome of the Taj Mahal. This was not the only building that he had constructed during his reign. He had built a marble palace for himself in each of the three main cities of his kingdom – Agra, Delhi and Lahore. To do this he had pulled down many of the existing buildings of Akbar's red sandstone fort. Later in his reign, after Mumtaz Mahal died, he made Delhi his capital and founded a whole new city called Shahjahanabad. Here he built himself a fort near the river surrounded by a massive red sandstone wall, just like the one his grandfather, Akbar, had built at Agra. Then there had been his famous peacock throne made of solid gold. Twelve pillars of emerald held up its canopy and above, were two peacocks, their tails made from sapphires and emeralds. Between these birds stood a tree, its branches dripping diamond and ruby fruit. But all these riches were now forgotten by the old Shah Jahan, content to be silent and look at the distant marble face of the Taj Mahal while a small brown mouse crouched at his feet, nibbling pomegranate seeds.

AURANGZEB'S BETRAYAL

His mind turned towards his son, Aurangzeb's betrayal and the events which had led to his imprisonment. But he thought of all these things as if they had happened a long time ago; almost as if he were watching them from a great distance. His voice, when it broke the silence, was no more than a whisper. He spoke only to himself, forgetting even the presence of the little mouse.

"I was haunted, haunted even at the height of my power by thoughts of how I, as a favourite son, had gone into battle against my father. I was determined to stop the same thing happening to me. I had four sons, but Dara was my favourite. I knew how worried I had felt by being always sent far from court to fight distant battles and it was this worry that had led to my final rebellion. So I kept Dara close to me and lavished him with gifts and attention. He was always more interested in poetry, books and music than battle and so he was suited to life at court. It was Aurangzeb who I sent south, time and time again on dangerous campaigns. In this I made a great mistake, for he learned many valuable lessons in the art of warfare. When the moment arose, he was the best able of my sons to return at the head of an army and seize the crown.

*Picture of Shah Jahan
and his four sons*

SHAH JAHAN: THE STORY OF THE TAJ MAHAL

"Now I can see that I often treated Aurangzeb unfairly. He was a good soldier and yet I never praised him for his talents. Instead, I found much in him to criticise. I accused him of greed when he asked for more money to administer to the poor areas in the south that he had subdued. I disregarded his advice, and was never generous in my gifts to him. He has behaved undutifully to me, he has betrayed me, but even as I sit as his prisoner, I wonder if I can entirely blame him.

"When, at the age of fifty-seven, I first fell seriously ill and retired to this fort at Agra, I handed the control of the government over to Dara. Each of his three brothers then prepared to march on Delhi with an army to contest the throne. I had recovered my health to some extent and wanted to prevent battle by talking to all my sons. But Dara decided to go to into battle with Aurangzeb. It was a hot day when the two armies met just outside Agra, so hot that the soldiers skins blistered beneath their armour. Dara was an inexperienced soldier and although he had many trained men and ranks of elephants, he was defeated and had to flee for his life back to Agra. He was too ashamed to see me and remained shut away until the next morning when he escaped from the city with his wife and children, riding on horses and elephants. I sent mules after him laden with gold coins, but I was never to see him again.

"Agra was now surrounded by Aurangzeb's troops. I made some attempt to make peace with him, presenting him with the famous sword called the Alamgir which means 'Seizer of the Universe', but the misunderstandings between us were too great.

His troops seized the gate to the Jumna river and stopped any fresh water passing into the fort. The wells which had not been used for years, were bitter and almost undrinkable. After three days I surrendered and my son entered the city and ordered my imprisonment. It was a year later that Aurangzeb captured Dara and brought him back to Delhi with his fifteen year old son, Sipihr Shukoh. There he made them ride through the streets, dressed in rags, sitting on a thin old elephant. A slave sat behind them with a sword ready to cut their heads off if they tried to escape. Soon afterwards, Dara was brutally killed in his prison and I was sent news of this. I had only my beautiful Jahanara to comfort me. Further news was brought to me of the deaths of my son Murad, my grandson and great grandsons, murdered and poisoned under Aurangzeb's orders."

THE DEATH OF SHAH JAHAN

THE old man, Shah Jahan paused. He breathed in deeply and the air shuddered as it entered his lungs. "So much death, so much death," he muttered. "All for a throne, all for a power that must come to an end. It cannot last and this Aurangzeb will learn. Either through violent death or old age he will come to realise that no one can hold on to the things of this world. When it is my time to die, and I feel that that time is close now, I know that I will at least have left behind me something of pure beauty. When I look from this window and see the shining perfection of the Taj Mahal, I see in it the best of myself. All my jewels, all my conquests, and all my power pale in comparison and are nothing compared to it. It is for this that I will be remembered and that my name will be written in history. I will not be known as Shah Jahan the soldier, the destroyer of his enemies, but as the man who created the Taj Mahal. In this way my love for my Mumtaz Mahal will last forever. This building was my offering to her, to India and to God."

Shah Jahan now sat quite peacefully, a soft smile on his lips. It was like this that his daughter, Jahanara found him. She uttered a small cry when she saw the spilled fruit and she knelt to pick it up. There was no sign of the small brown mouse. He had eaten his fill of fruit and carried away a few seeds to his family hidden away in a carefully concealed hole in the corner of the room. Jahanara chatted to her father as she cleared away the fruit, repeating a poem she had recently read, trying to distract him from any worrying thoughts. Then she felt his hand touch her shoulder lightly. She looked up and he touched her cheek. Softly he said, "I forgive him. Tell your brother, Aurangzeb, I pardon him." Then Shah Jahan became quite still, but a peaceful smile remained on his face. Jahanara realised that her father had died. The next morning his body was taken across the water of the Jumna to his final resting place in the Taj Mahal, next to his beloved wife, Mumtaz Mahal. ~

TREASURES FROM THE EAST SERIES

Ibn Tulun: The Story of a Mosque
Shah Jahan & The Story of the Taj Mahal

Forthcoming Autumn 1996
In the City of Suleiman the Magnificent